Our Perfect Wedding day

....

&

....

IF FOUND, PLEASE RETURN TO:

Name:

Address:

Cell Phone: FAX:

Work Phone: FAX:

Primary E-Mail:

Secondary E-Mail:

There is no more lovely, friendly, and charming relationship, communion or company than a good marriage.

— Martin Luther

Save the Date

Wedding Date

Ceremony Venue

Program

Time

Wedding Checklist

12 months before

Notes

- ☐ Engagement Announcement
- ☐ Find and Reserve Venue
- ☐ Decide on a budget
- ☐ Set your dream wedding date
- ☐ Choose bridesmaid & Groomsmen
- ☐ Book phographer & Videographer
- ☐ Find and book Officiant
- ☐ Choose wedding theme & style
- ☐ Begin shopping for wedding dress
- ☐ Book Caterer & Bartender
- ☐ Book Florist & Entertainment
- ☐ Choose a seamstress for dress alterations
- ☐ Book transportation for wedding & reception
- ☐ Choose & order wedding invitations
- ☐ Shop for hair accessories, jewelry
- ☐ Shop for bridesmaid dresses & Groomsmen suits
- ☐ Make your Gift registry
- ☐ Make a draft guest list
- ☐ Research Bakery
- ☐ Research Honeymoon Destinations

Wedding Checklist

12-10 months before

Notes

- [ ] Engagement Announcement
- [ ] Find and Reserve Venue
- [ ] Decide on a budget
- [ ] Set your dream wedding date
- [ ] Choose bridesmaid & Groomsmen
- [ ] Book phographer & Videographer
- [ ] Find and book Officiant
- [ ] Choose wedding theme & style
- [ ] Begin shopping for wedding dress
- [ ] Book Caterer & Bartender
- [ ] Book Florist & Entertainment
- [ ] Choose a seamstress for dress alterations
- [ ] Book transportation for wedding & reception
- [ ] Choose & order wedding invitations
- [ ] Shop for hair accessories, jewelry
- [ ] Shop for bridesmaid dresses & Groomsmen suits
- [ ] Apply for Passports
- [ ] Make a draft guest list
- [ ] Research Bakery
- [ ] Research Honeymoon Destinations

Wedding Checklist

9-7 months before

Notes

- ☐ Plan & book your Honeymoon
- ☐ Make your Gift Registry
- ☐ Have a meeting with Officiant
- ☐ Shop for shoes & accessories
- ☐ Book your wedding night Hotel room
- ☐ Complete Guest List
- ☐ Collect Guest addresses
- ☐ Reserve hotel rooms for out of town guests
- ☐ Discuss ceremony details
- ☐ Order wedding cake
- ☐ Get with maid of honour to discuss bachelorette party
- ☐ Choose a seamstress for dress alterations
- ☐ Begin shopping for wedding party dresses+ suits
- ☐ Research for makeup & hair artists

Wedding Checklist

6-5 months before

- [ ] Send out save the date cards
- [ ] Order the cake
- [ ] Order favors
- [ ] Purchase the wedding rings
- [ ] Review proofs of wedding invitations
- [ ] Finalize guest list
- [ ] Reserve rental items for ceremony & reception
- [ ] Revisit the wedding budget to stay on track
- [ ] Decide the menu
- [ ] Choose gifts for wedding party
- [ ] Purchase a garter
- [ ] Finalize place & time for rehearsal dinner
- [ ] Meet vendors to finalize all selections
- [ ] Choose ceremony reading

Notes

....
....
....
....
....
....
....
....
....
....
....
....
....
....
....
....

Wedding Checklist

4-2 months before

Notes

- ☐ Trial run on hair & makeup artists
- ☐ Finalize menu with caterer
- ☐ Begin to write your vows
- ☐ Send the wedding invitation
- ☐ Purchase wedding party gifts
- ☐ Purchase cake knife & stand
- ☐ Confirm ceremony running order with officiant
- ☐ Send the draft run sheets to vendors
- ☐ Obtain wedding license
- ☐ Purchase guest book
- ☐ Start dance lessons
- ☐ Request leave from work
- ☐ Finalize flowers & centerpieces
- ☐ Bridal shower
- ☐ Find shoes for groom & groomsmen
- ☐ Arrange alcohol services

Wedding Checklist

2-1 months before

Notes

- ☐ Finalize wedding day schedule
- ☐ Finalize guest list again
- ☐ Choose wedding music
- ☐ Obtain wedding license, if not done so
- ☐ Start seating chart
- ☐ Purchase place cards
- ☐ Confirm & finalize vendors
- ☐ Choose date for bachelorette night
- ☐ Collect the RSVP cards and assure attendance
- ☐ Have final wedding outfit fitting
- ☐ Enjoy your bachelorette
- ☐ Finalize payments to vendors
- ☐ Finalize complete decor

Wedding Checklist

1 week Before

Notes

- ☐ Inform caterer of the final guest count
- ☐ Organize your wedding day attire
- ☐ Try on your shoes(or they will hurt that night)
- ☐ Waxing , threading, tanning, mani, pedi,hair dying
- ☐ Prepare checks for vendors
- ☐ Confirm rehearsal dinner reservation
- ☐ Confirm hotel reservations for out of town guests
- ☐ Confirm drop off times & locations with all vendors
- ☐ Have the engagement rings cleaned professionally
- ☐ Finalize your vows
- ☐ Gather all travel documents for your honeymoon
- ☐ Pack your honeymoon

Wedding Checklist

1-3 days Before

Notes

- ☐ Rehearse ceremony
- ☐ Arrange pick up transportations for guests without cars
- ☐ Give gifts to attendants at rehearsal dinner
- ☐ Deliver table cards, menu & favors to venue
- ☐ Give marriage license to the officiant
- ☐ Steam wedding and bridesmaid dress
- ☐ Now Relax, you have everything prepared
- ☐ Now enjoy the moment

Wedding Checklist

The Big Day

- [ ] Give gifts to parents
- [ ] Give bands to maid of honour/ Best man
- [ ] Enjoy your day
- [ ] Go marry your best friend

Notes

....
....
....
....
....
....
....
....
....
....
....
....
....
....
....
....
....

WEDDING DATE .... BUDGET .... COLOUR SCHEME ....

STYLE: VINTAGE / ROMANTIC / CLASSIC / RETRO / MODERN / OTHER ....

WEDDING CEREMONY

CEREMONY LOCATION .... CEREMONY TIME .... TO ....

ADDRESS .... NUMBER OF GUESTS ....

WEDDING RECEPTION

RECEPTION LOCATION .... RECEPTION TIME .... TO ....

ADDRESS .... NUMBER OF GUESTS ....

BRIDESMAIDS | GROOMS

IMPORTANT DATES

ENGAGEMENT PARTY .... TO ....
BRIDAL SHOWER .... TO ....
BACHELOR PARTY .... TO ....
REHEARSAL DINNER .... TO ....
BRIDAL SHOWER .... TO ....
HONEYMOON .... TO ....

Wedding Contact

WEDDING PLANNER

Name:
Address:

Phone:
Web:

RECEPTION VENUE

Name:
Address:

Phone:
Web:

CEREMONY VENUE

Name:
Address:

Phone:
Web:

OFFICIANT

Name:
Address:

Phone:
Web:

PHOTOGRAPHER

Name:
Address:

Phone:
Web:

VIDEOGRAPHER

Name:
Address:

Phone:
Web:

Wedding Contact

FLORIST

Name:
Address:

Phone:
Web:

BAKER

Name:
Address:

Phone:
Web:

CATERER

Name:
Address:

Phone:
Web:

TRANSPORTATION

Name:
Address:

Phone:
Web:

DJ/ ENTERTAINMENT

Name:
Address:

Phone:
Web:

LIGHTING COMPANY

Name:
Address:

Phone:
Web:

Wedding Contact

BRIDAL DRESS

Name:
Address:

Phone:
Web:

MAKEUP ARTIST

Name:
Address:

Phone:
Web:

HAIR STYLIST

Name:
Address:

Phone:
Web:

JEWELER

Name:
Address:

Phone:
Web:

STATIONARY DESIGNER

Name:
Address:

Phone:
Web:

HONEYMOON RESORT

Name:
Address:

Phone:
Web:

Order of Events

PRIORITY	DATE & TIME	EVENT	SONG

Order of Events

PRIORITY	DATE & TIME	EVENT	SONG

Order of Events

PRIORITY	DATE & TIME	EVENT	SONG

Order of Events

PRIORITY	DATE & TIME	EVENT	SONG

Order of Events

PRIORITY	DATE & TIME	EVENT	SONG

Dates to Remember

Notes:

Dates to Remember

Notes:

Dates to Remember

Notes:

Dates to Remember

Notes:
_____
_____
_____
_____

Song List

EVENT	SONG	ARTIST	VERSION

Song List

EVENT	SONG	ARTIST	VERSION

Song List

EVENT	SONG	ARTIST	VERSION

Guest List

NAME	CONTACT INFORMATION	RSVP
		☐
		☐
		☐
		☐
		☐
		☐
		☐
		☐
		☐
		☐
		☐

Guest List

NAME	CONTACT INFORMATION	RSVP
		☐
		☐
		☐
		☐
		☐
		☐
		☐
		☐
		☐
		☐
		☐

Guest List

NAME	CONTACT INFORMATION	RSVP
		☐
		☐
		☐
		☐
		☐
		☐
		☐
		☐
		☐
		☐

NAME	CONTACT INFORMATION	RSVP
		☐
		☐
		☐
		☐
		☐
		☐
		☐
		☐
		☐
		☐
		☐

Guest List

NAME	CONTACT INFORMATION	RSVP
		☐
		☐
		☐
		☐
		☐
		☐
		☐
		☐
		☐
		☐
		☐

Guest List

NAME	CONTACT INFORMATION	RSVP
		☐
		☐
		☐
		☐
		☐
		☐
		☐
		☐
		☐
		☐
		☐

Guest List

NAME	CONTACT INFORMATION	RSVP
		☐
		☐
		☐
		☐
		☐
		☐
		☐
		☐
		☐
		☐

Seating Chart

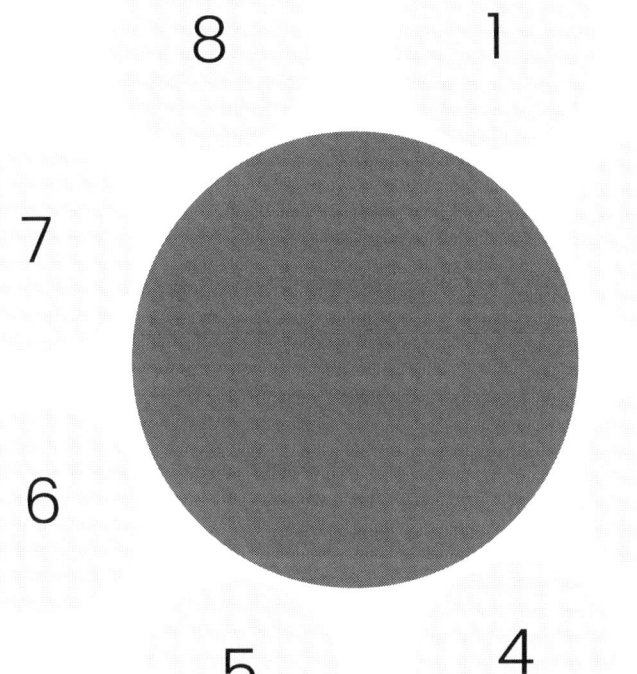

TABLE NO.1

1.
2.
3.
4.
5.
6.
7.
8.

TABLE NO.2

1.
2.
3.
4.
5.
6.
7.
8.

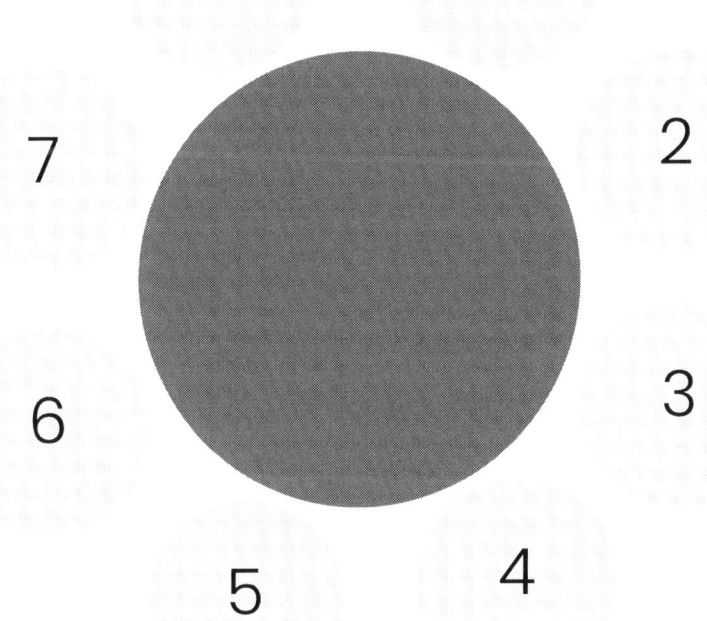

Seating Chart

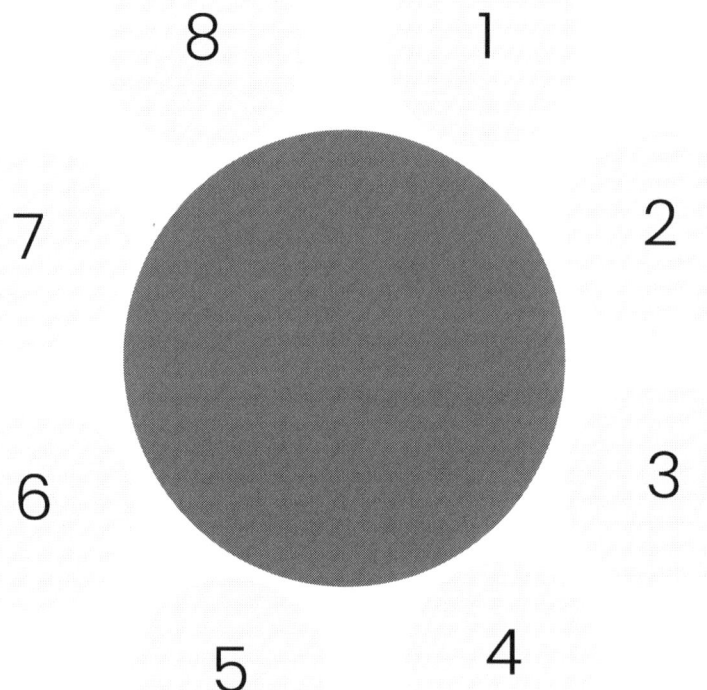

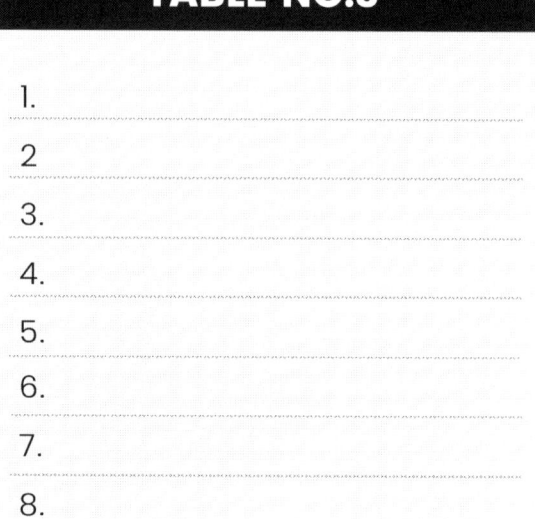

TABLE NO.3

1.
2.
3.
4.
5.
6.
7.
8.

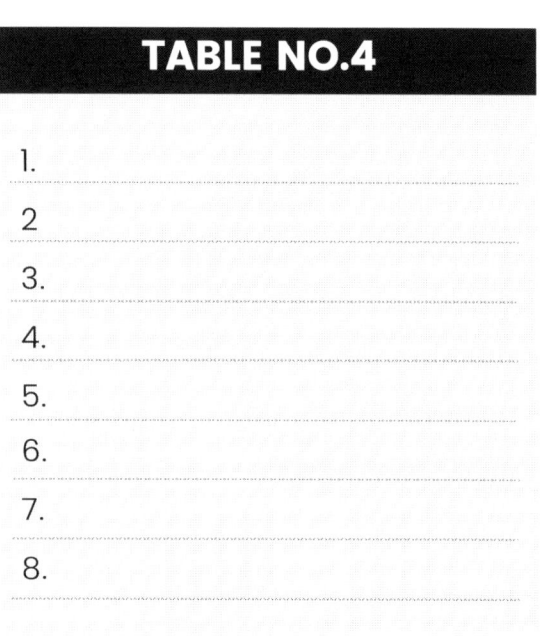

TABLE NO.4

1.
2.
3.
4.
5.
6.
7.
8.

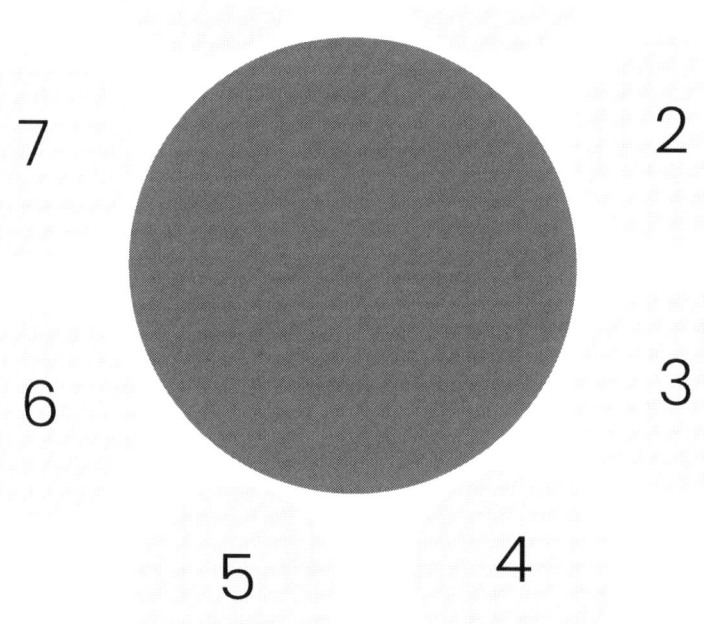

Seating Chart

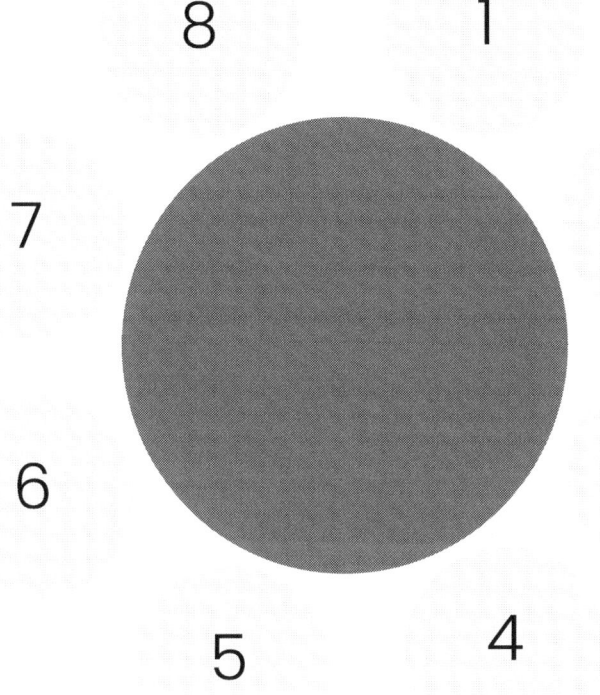

TABLE NO.5

1.
2.
3.
4.
5.
6.
7.
8.

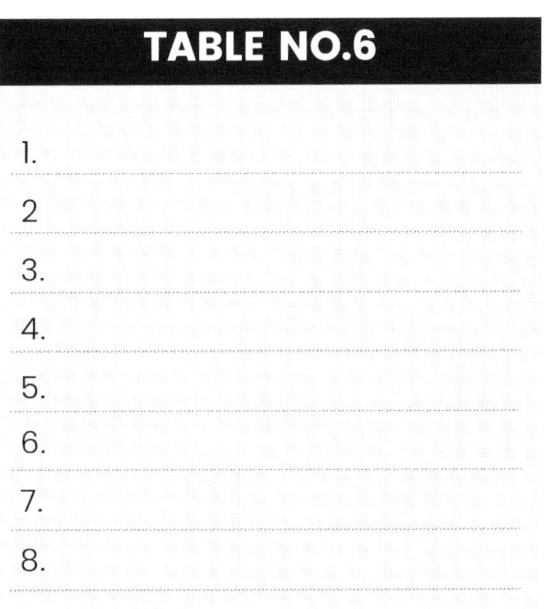

TABLE NO.6

1.
2.
3.
4.
5.
6.
7.
8.

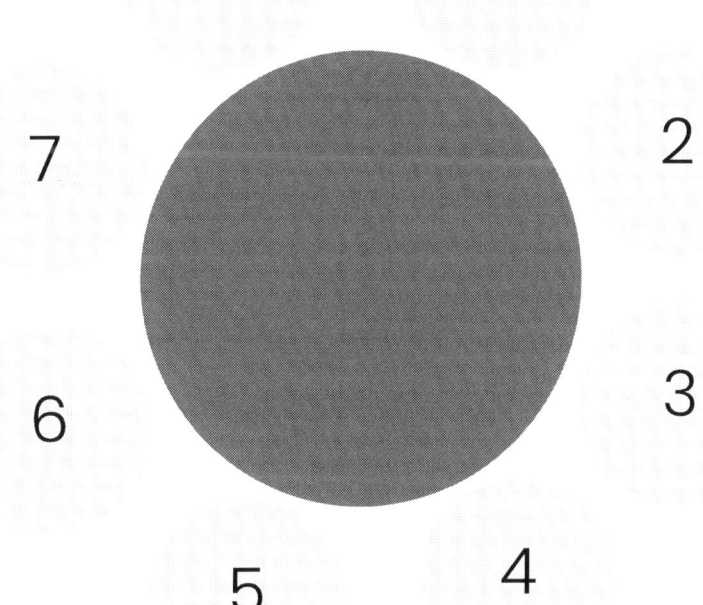

Seating Chart

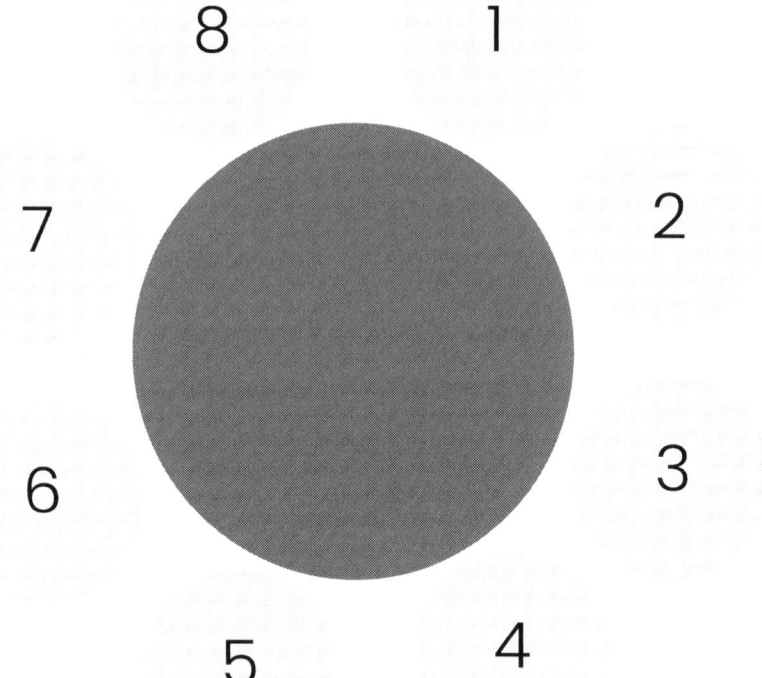

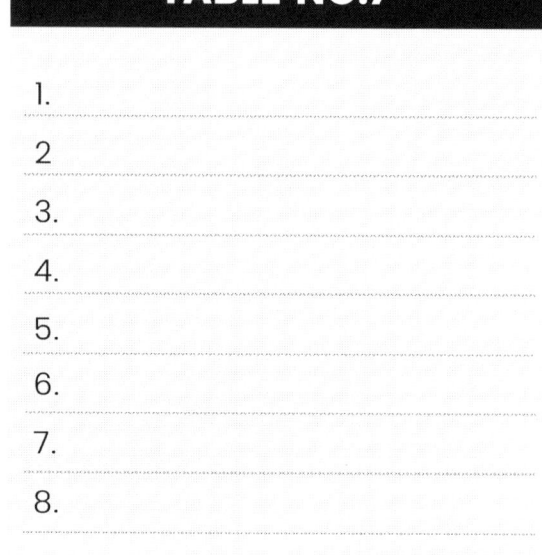

TABLE NO.7

1.
2.
3.
4.
5.
6.
7.
8.

TABLE NO.8

1.
2.
3.
4.
5.
6.
7.
8.

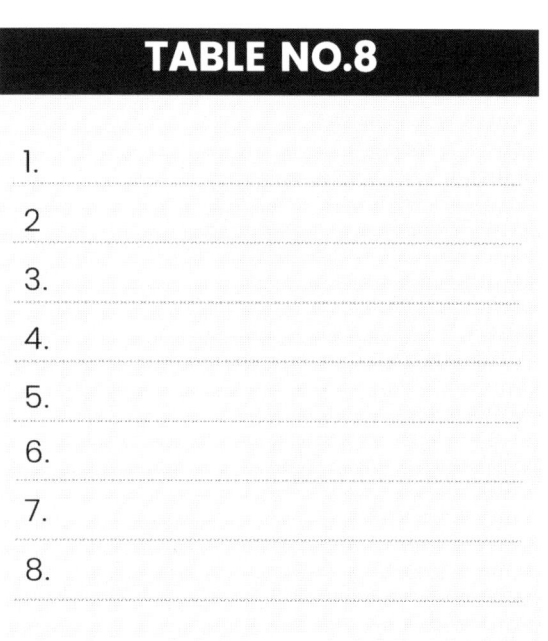

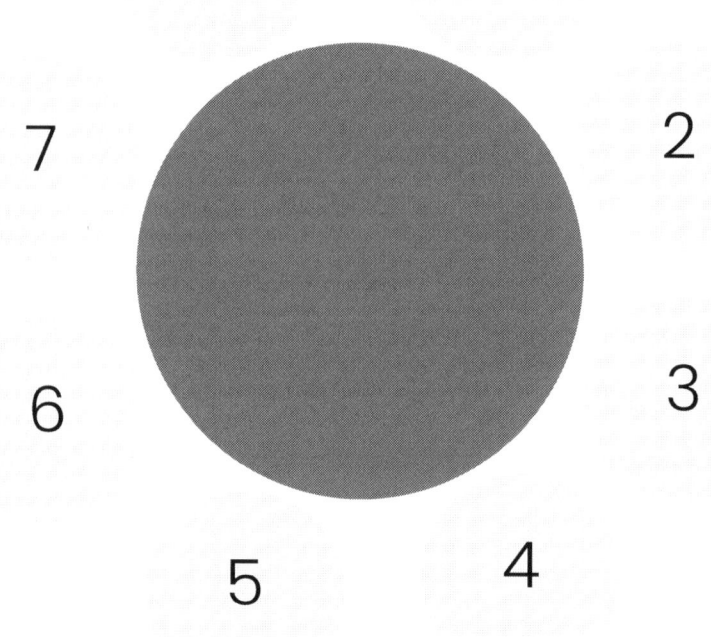

Seating Chart

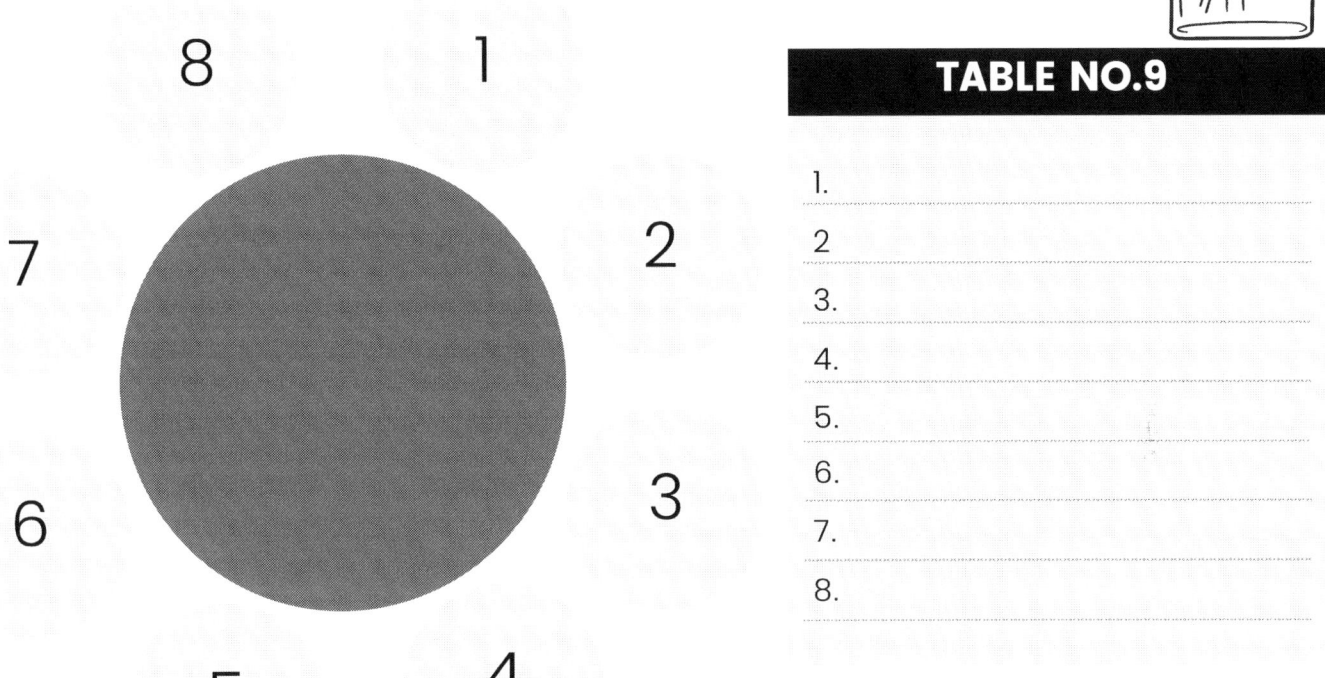

TABLE NO.9

1.
2.
3.
4.
5.
6.
7.
8.

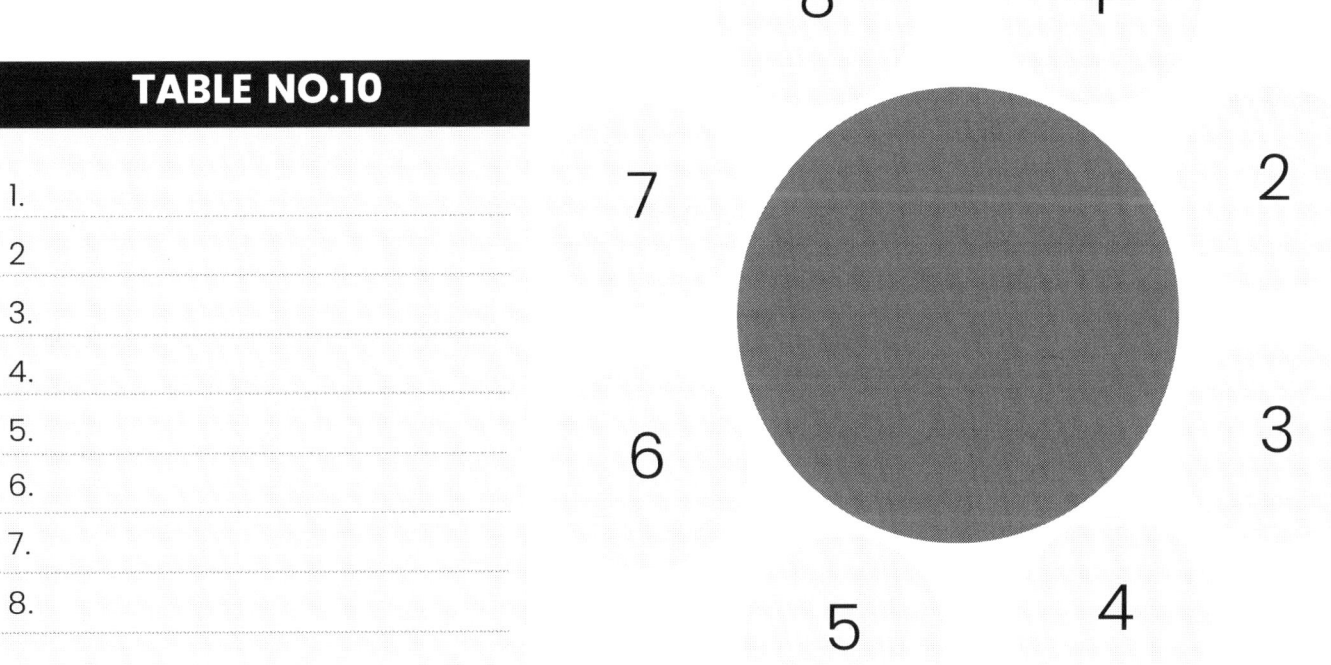

TABLE NO.10

1.
2.
3.
4.
5.
6.
7.
8.

Seating Chart

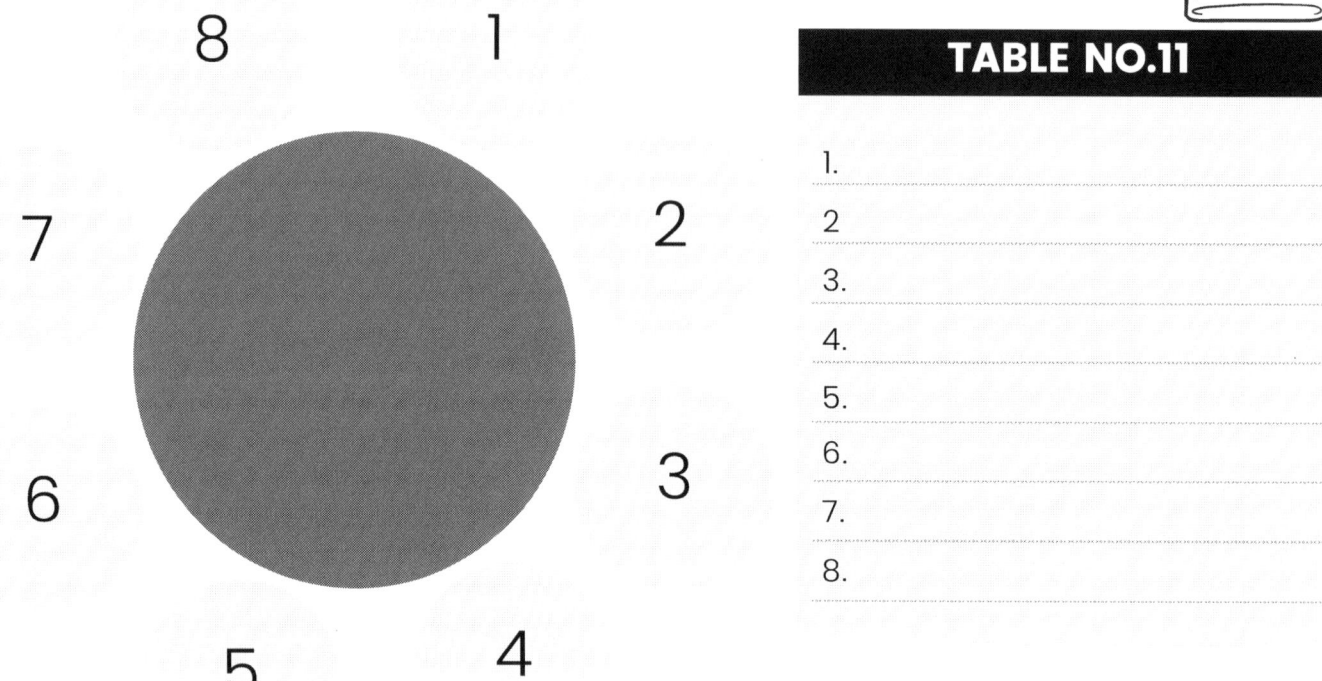

TABLE NO.11

1.
2.
3.
4.
5.
6.
7.
8.

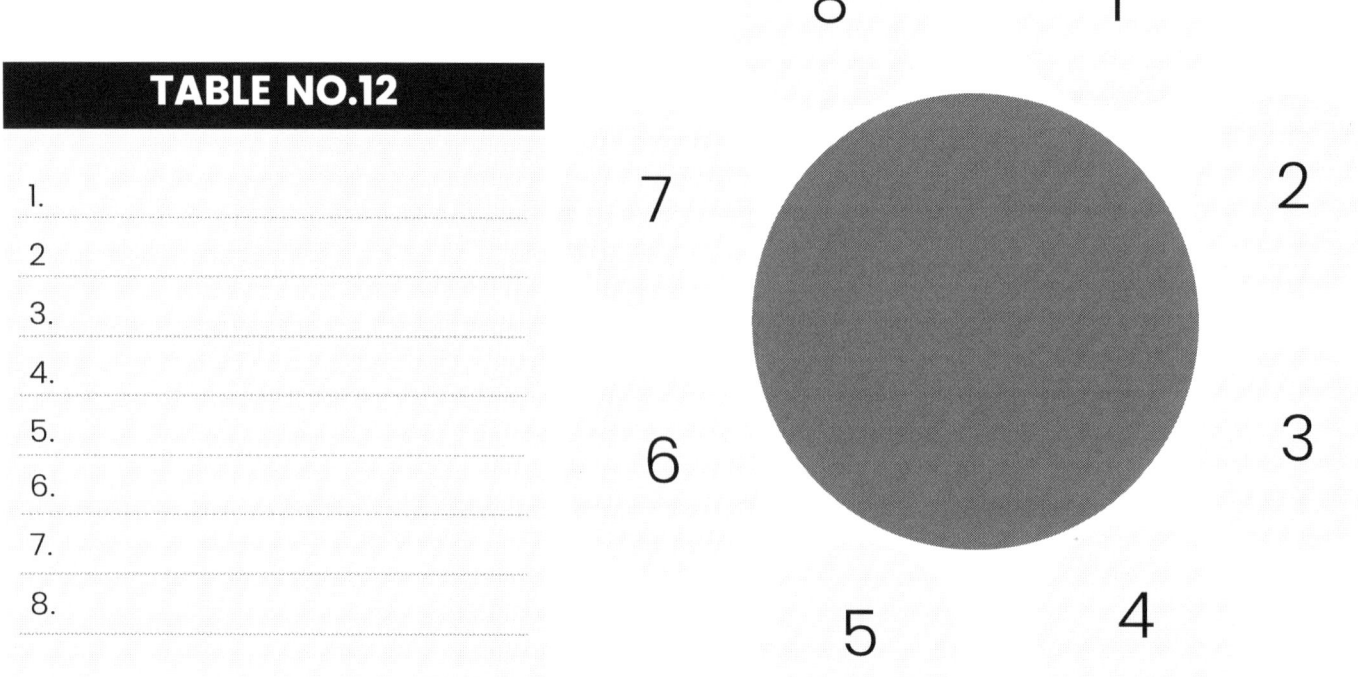

TABLE NO.12

1.
2.
3.
4.
5.
6.
7.
8.

Seating Chart

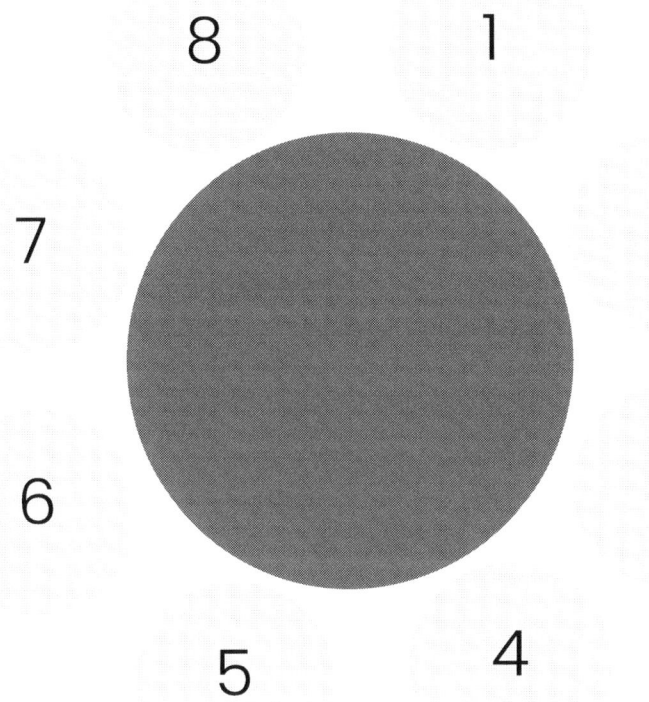

TABLE NO.13

1.
2.
3.
4.
5.
6.
7.
8.

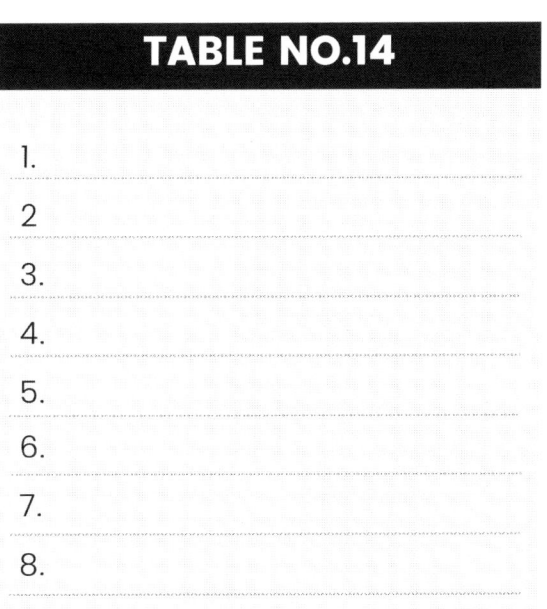

TABLE NO.14

1.
2.
3.
4.
5.
6.
7.
8.

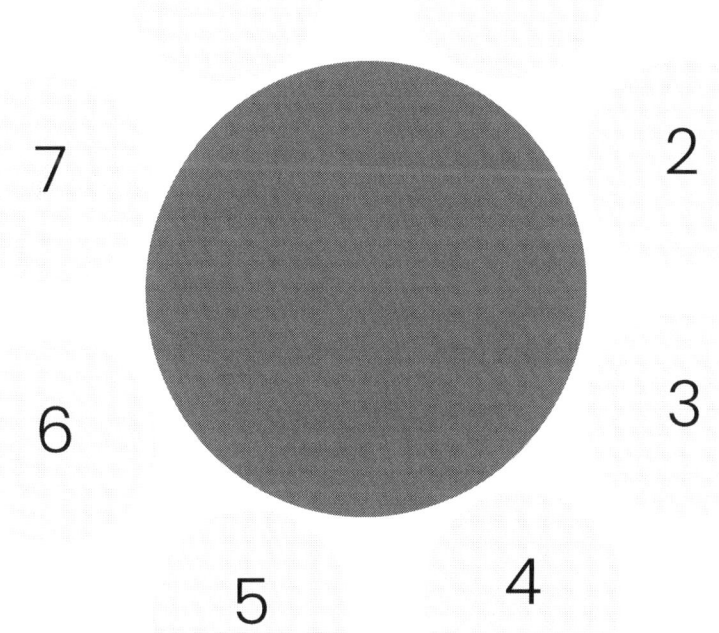

Seating Chart

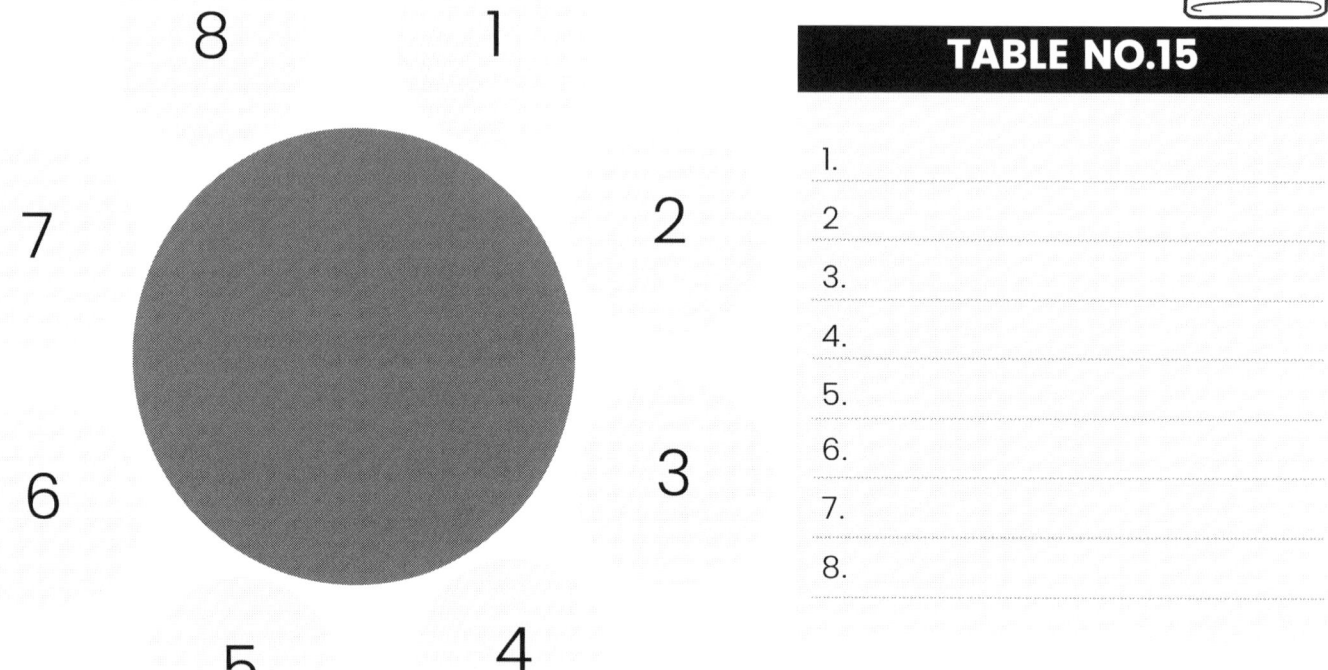

TABLE NO.15

1.
2.
3.
4.
5.
6.
7.
8.

TABLE NO.16

1.
2.
3.
4.
5.
6.
7.
8.

Seating Chart

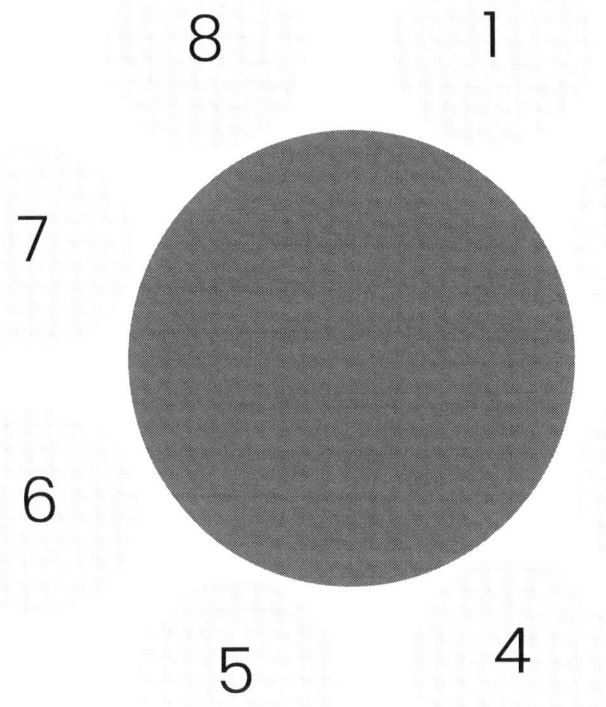

TABLE NO.17

1.
2.
3.
4.
5.
6.
7.
8.

TABLE NO.18

1.
2.
3.
4.
5.
6.
7.
8.

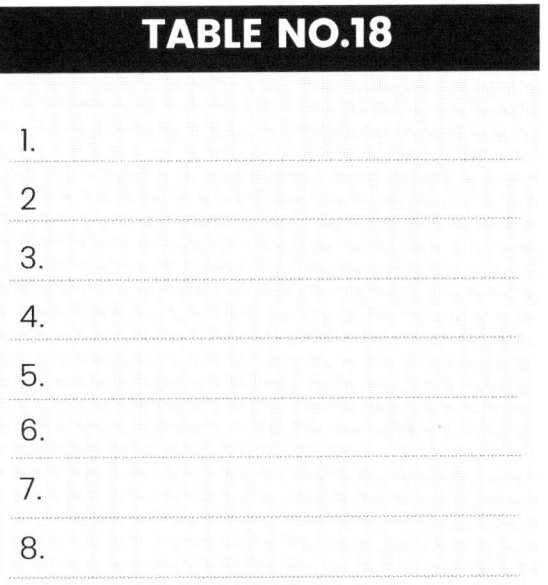

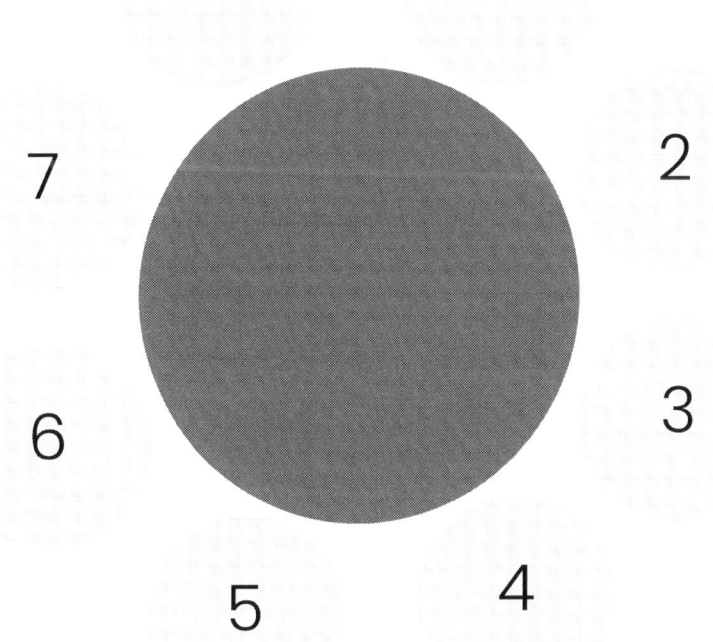

Seating Chart

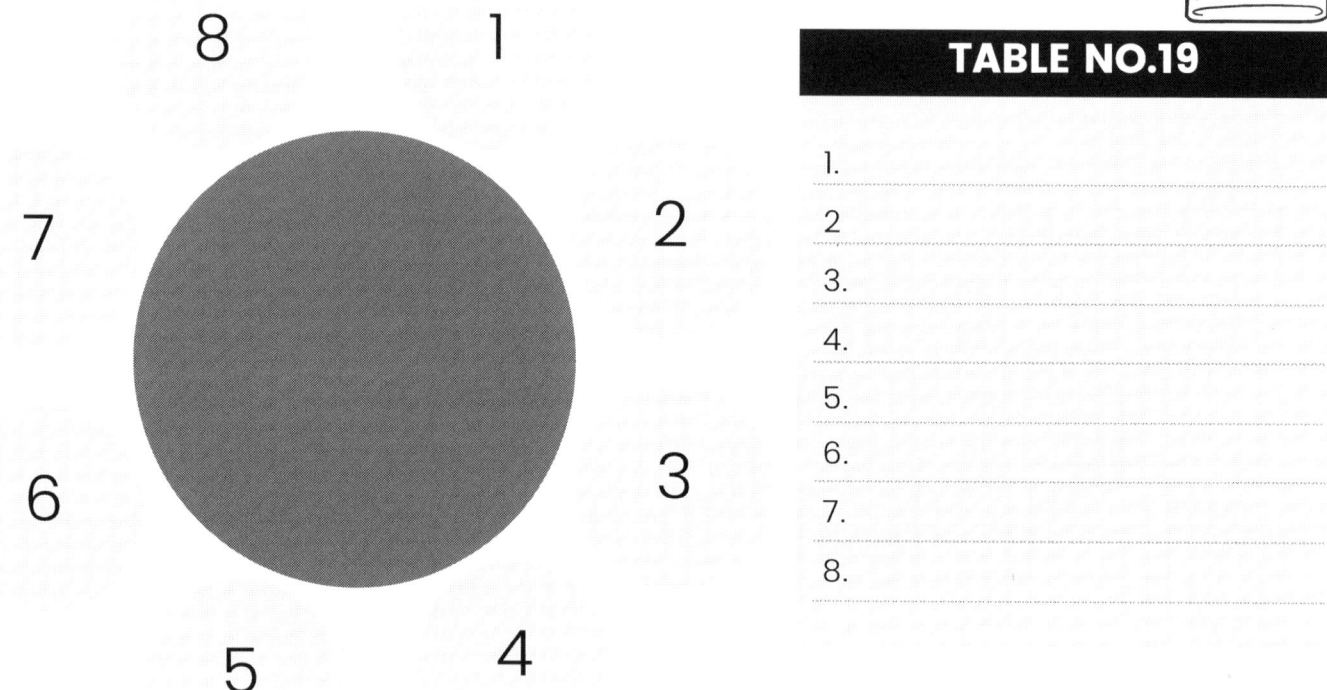

TABLE NO.19

1.
2.
3.
4.
5.
6.
7.
8.

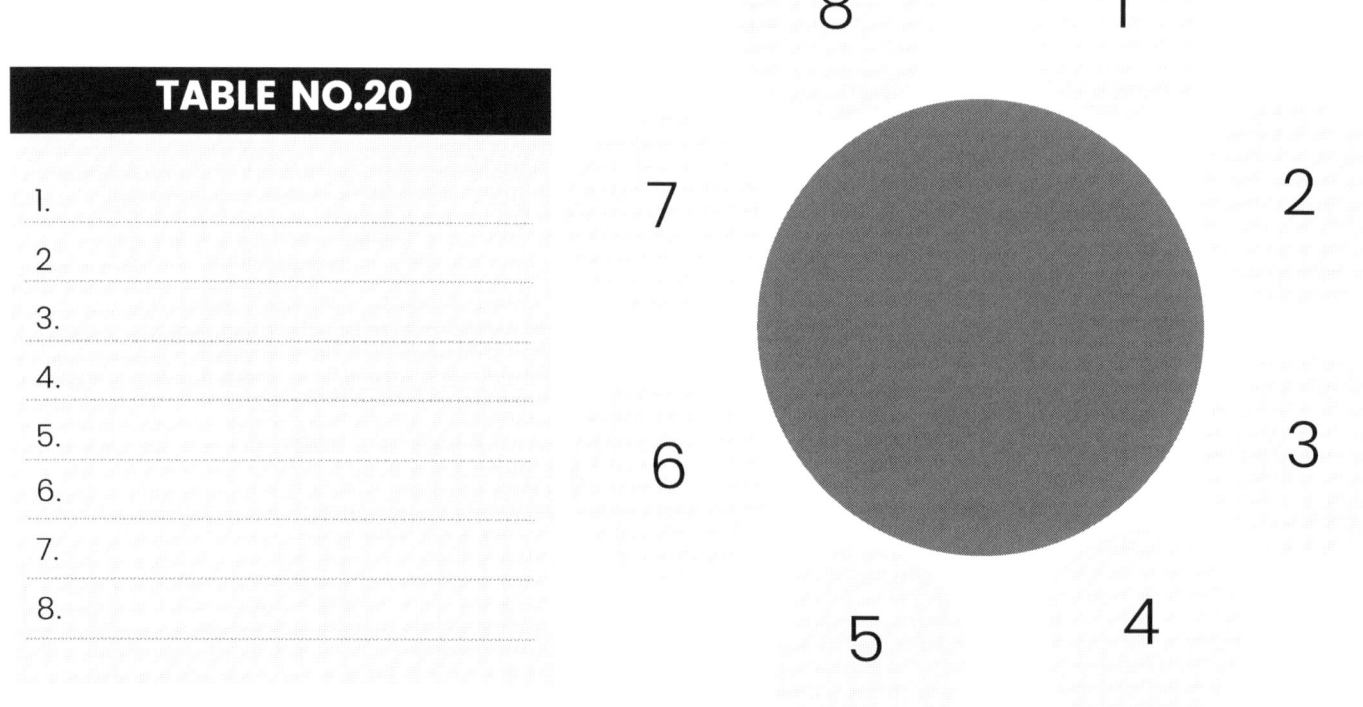

TABLE NO.20

1.
2.
3.
4.
5.
6.
7.
8.

Wedding Attire Budget

Item	Budget	Spent	Paid
Engagement Party Outfit (plus shoes and accessories)			
Engagement Photos Outfit (plus shoes and accessories)			
Bridal shower Outfit (plus shoes and accessories)			
Bachelor/ Bachelorette Outfit (plus shoes and accessories)			
Rehersal dinner Outfit (plus shoes and accessories)			
Wedding dress			
Wedding dress Alterations			
Speciality Undergarments			
Veil, Wedding Shoes, and Bridal Jewelry/ Accessories			
Groom's Tux + Shoes			
Reception outfit (if you're changing out your dress) or after party outfit			
Post-wedding Brunch Outfit (plus shoe and accessories)			
Wedding Dress cleaning & press reservation			

NOTES

Wedding Beauty Budget

Item	Budget	Spent	Paid
Pre-Wedding Haircuts or Color			
Waxing			
Facial			
Mani-Pedi			
Professional Shave			
Tips (normally around 20 % for any pre wedding beauty treatments)			
Spray Tan			
Lash Extensions			
Hair trial Appointments			
Day of wedding Hairstyle			
Makeup Trial Appointment			
Day of Wedding makeup			

NOTES

Wedding Cake Budget

Item	Budget	Spent	Paid
Cake Display/ Cake Cutting			
Sheet Cake for extra servings			
Speciality Design Elements (like sugar flowers or hand painting)			
Cake Topper			
Cake Stand			
Cake-Cutting Fee			
Delivery Fee			
Additional deserts (if you're doing a desert table/station)			
Preservation Kit for one year anniversary			

NOTES

Wedding Ceremony Budget

Item	Budget	Spent	Paid
Ceremony Site (if seperate from reception venue			
Church Donation			
Officiant Fee			
Marriage License			
Ceremony accessories (ring pillow, flower girl basket, unity candles etc.)			

NOTES

Wedding Drinks Budget

Item	Budget	Spent	Paid
Cocktail Hour Drinks			
Reception Drinks			
Champagne Toast			
Open Bar/ Hosted Beer & Wine Speciality Cocktails			
Bartender Service			
Mixers			
Coffee/ Tea			
Non- alcoholic Beverages			
Glassware (if not included in your catering package)			
Bar Signage			
Corkage Fees			
Liquor License (if not provided by venue or caterer			
Bartender Gratuity			

NOTES

Wedding Flowers Budget

Item	Budget	Spent	Paid
Bouquets (for bride and brides-maids and perhaps a toss bouquet)			
Boutonnieres (for groom, groomsmen, fathers and or grandfathers)			
Corsages for Mothers and GrandMothers			
Flowers and Accessories for the Flower Girl / Ring Bearer			
Ceremony Arch			
Ceremony Arrangements			
Reception Centerpieces for guest tables, guest book table, food station etc.			
Wedding Cake Flowers (If additional cake decor is needed)			
Wedding Chalkboards / Signage			
Speciality Decor rentals (e.g. Tenting, Lanterns, candlebras, etc.			
Delivery Fees			

NOTES

Wedding Food Budget

Item	Budget	Spent	Paid
Tasting appointment (if not complimentary with your catering package			
Rehearsal Dinner			
Passed Hors D'oeuvres			
Plated, Buffet, or Family-style meal			
Food Stations			
Service Staff			
Catering Equipment (such as plates, silverware, glassware, serving platters, etc.)			
Catering Rentals (such as tables, chairs, linens, etc.)			
Vendors Meals (it's nice to feed your photographer)			
Tax Gratuity (sometimes called the service charge)			
Set up and Clean up Fees			
Bar, Beverage service (see Drinks above, may be included in your catering package)			

NOTES

Wedding Invitations and Paper Budget

Item	Budget	Spent	Paid
Engagemnt Party Invitations			
Save the Date			
Wedding Invitations (including inserts like RSVP cards or maps)			
Rehearsal Dinner Invitations			
Post Wedding Brunch Invitations			
Envelopes (note that speciality size envelopes will be more expensive to ship)			
Postage (for Invitations & RSVP envelopes, as well ass thank you card)			
Return Address Labels			
Wedding ceremony programs			
Wedding Reception paper Goods			
Escort Cards			
Place Cards			
Menu Cards			
Custom Napkins			
Favor Lables			
Thank You Cards			

NOTES

Wedding DJ and Gifts Budget

Item	Budget	Spent	Paid
Wedding Favors			
Wedding Party Gifts			
Gifts for your Flower Girl or Ring Bearer			
House Gift			
Parents Gift			
Welcome Baskets for out of town Guests			
Ceremony Musicians			
Cocktail Hour Music			
Reception DJ or Live Band			
Microphone (for wedding ceremony and reception toasts)			
Sound-system or extra speakers			
Photo Booth & Dance Floor Lights (in case want to add this)			

NOTES

Wedding Photography & Videography Budget

Item	Budget	Spent	Paid
Session			
Rehearsal Dinner Coverage			
Day Coverage			
Albums or Prints			
Same Day Edits			
Raw Footage			
Highlight Reels			
Feature Film			

NOTES

Wedding Reception Budget

Item	Budget	Spent	Paid
Room Rental Fee			
Venue Deposit			
Ceremony Fee (If ceremony is being held at Reception Venue			
Additonal Rentals (such as table, chairs, china etc. if not provided by Caterers)			
Dance Floor Rental (If not Already Installed)			
Parking Fees			
Liablility Insurance			
Tax and Service Fees			
Security (some Venue Require it)			

NOTES

Wedding Transportation & Planner Budget

Item	Budget	Spent	Paid
Bridal Party Transportation to the ceremony Venue			
Bridal Party Transportation to the Reception Venue(If different from ceremony site)			
Gratuity for the Driver			
Shuttle Service to transport guests to / from their hotels			
Valet Parking Service			
Day of the Month or Full service wedding coordination			
Venue and/ or Vendor Referrals and Liaisons			
Budget Development			
Timeline Creation			
Rehearsal Coordination			
Wedding Day Set up & Management			

NOTES

Wedding Rings And Fund Budget

Item	Budget	Spent	Paid
Bands			
Band Resizing fee			
Ring Insurance			
Any Customization			
Vendor Tips			
Sales Tax			
Service Charges			
Wedding Insurance			
Miscelleneous Charges			
Ring cleaning Charges			

NOTES

Wedding Budget

DETAILS	ESTIMATES	COST	DEPOSIT	LEFT

Wedding Budget

DETAILS	ESTIMATES	COST	DEPOSIT	LEFT

DETAILS	ESTIMATES	COST	DEPOSIT	LEFT

DETAILS	ESTIMATES	COST	DEPOSIT	LEFT

Wedding Budget

DETAILS	ESTIMATES	COST	DEPOSIT	LEFT

Wedding Budget

DETAILS	ESTIMATES	COST	DEPOSIT	LEFT

Wedding Budget

DETAILS	ESTIMATES	COST	DEPOSIT	LEFT

Wedding Budget

DETAILS	ESTIMATES	COST	DEPOSIT	LEFT

Notes

Notes

Notes

Notes

Notes

Notes

Notes

Notes

Notes

To Do List

To Do List

To Do List

♡ ....

♡ ....

♡ ....

♡ ....

♡ ....

♡ ....

♡ ....

♡ ....

♡ ....

♡ ....

♡ ....

To Do List

- ♡ ....
- ♡ ....
- ♡ ....
- ♡ ....
- ♡ ....
- ♡ ....
- ♡ ....
- ♡ ....
- ♡ ....
- ♡ ....
- ♡ ....

To Do List

- ♡ ....
- ♡ ....
- ♡ ....
- ♡ ....
- ♡ ....
- ♡ ....
- ♡ ....
- ♡ ....
- ♡ ....
- ♡ ....
- ♡ ....

To Do List

- ♡ ....
- ♡ ....
- ♡ ....
- ♡ ....
- ♡ ....
- ♡ ....
- ♡ ....
- ♡ ....
- ♡ ....
- ♡ ....
- ♡ ....

To Do List

- ♡ ....
- ♡ ....
- ♡ ....
- ♡ ....
- ♡ ....
- ♡ ....
- ♡ ....
- ♡ ....
- ♡ ....
- ♡ ....
- ♡ ....

To Do List

♡ ....

♡ ....

♡ ....

♡ ....

♡ ....

♡ ....

♡ ....

♡ ....

♡ ....

♡ ....

♡ ....

To Do List

♡ ....

♡ ....

♡ ....

♡ ....

♡ ....

♡ ....

♡ ....

♡ ....

♡ ....

♡ ....

♡ ....

To Do List

- ♡ ....
- ♡ ....
- ♡ ....
- ♡ ....
- ♡ ....
- ♡ ....
- ♡ ....
- ♡ ....
- ♡ ....
- ♡ ....
- ♡ ....

To Do List

- ♡ ....
- ♡ ....
- ♡ ....
- ♡ ....
- ♡ ....
- ♡ ....
- ♡ ....
- ♡ ....
- ♡ ....
- ♡ ....
- ♡ ....

And they Lived Happily Ever After

Printed in Great Britain
by Amazon